Bubble-wrapped

Lorraine Gregory

Illustrated by **Chloe Douglass**

OXFORD
UNIVERSITY PRESS

Letter from the Author

I was raised on a council estate in East London by an Austrian mother and an Indian father. My love of reading and a wild imagination led to years of making up stories in my head, but none of them made it to the page until I began writing them down for my son.

I have lived with epilepsy for twenty-five years and I use medication to successfully manage my seizures.

My debut children's novel, *Mold and the Poison Plot*, won the SCBWI Crystal Kite award for UK and Ireland. My second book, *The Maker of Monsters*, was shortlisted for the FCBG Children's Book Award.

I live in the south of England with my family and two very fluffy cats.

Lorraine Gregory

Chapter One

'Have you got everything, Amy?' Mum asks, after she's finally managed to find a parking spot in the chaos of school drop-off.

'I think so,' Amy says, gathering all her bags together.

'Good girl. Now, are you sure you don't want me to come in with you?'

'I'll be fine, Mum. Stop worrying.' Amy opens the car door and gets out.

'All right, all right,' her mum says through the open window. 'Just have a wonderful day, take care and I'll be here at three for pick-up. OK?'

'Mum, I don't need a lift home. I can walk just fine.'

'I know you can, Amy love, but I want to. We can go and get cake at that new place on the way home as a treat, and you can tell me all about your first day!'

Amy manages to suppress a loud sigh. She knows her mum is trying to be nice but, just for once, she wants to enjoy her independence.

'All right Mum, thanks,' she says and is rewarded with a beaming smile which only makes her feel worse about what she's about to do. Finally, her mum drives away.

Amy waves until the car's out of sight then quickly takes off her medical-alert necklace and tucks it into her bag, ignoring the pang of guilt in her belly.

If she has to start a new school in the middle of the year then she's going to make the most out of being the girl no one knows. Now that she's on medication that actually works, she should easily be able to keep her epilepsy hidden from the other children. For once she can just be herself, Amy, not the girl who has seizures and has to wear a padded helmet everywhere in case she falls and hurts her head.

She hitches her bag onto her shoulder, takes a deep breath and prepares for a brand new start.

* * *

Amy can only get away with not telling everyone because her new IHP (Individual Health Plan) for school says her epilepsy is 'well controlled'. She remembers making her mum fill it in like that just after they moved.

'It's true!' she had insisted to her mum. 'I haven't had a seizure for months! The medication is working. The school and the teachers need to know about my epilepsy, but I don't need special treatment any more! *Please*, Mum.'

'Amy, I'm not sure.'

'I just want to feel normal,' Amy insisted. 'I don't want all the other children knowing I have epilepsy before I even start!'

'I just think we should be careful ... '

'I'm fed up of being careful!' Amy's voice broke and her mum could see just how upset she was. 'My whole life I've been careful. It feels like I've been wrapped in fifteen layers of bubble wrap and no one can ever see me. The *real* me.

Inside. All they can see is the bubble wrap.'

Amy's mum sighed and gently pushed Amy's hair behind her ear. 'All right, I'll tell you what. We'll tell the head teacher you have epilepsy that's well controlled with medication. We'll let them know you don't need extra help and prefer that it's not discussed with the other children if possible. *But*,' she holds up a finger, 'you *must* keep your medical-alert necklace on just in case.'

'Deal,' Amy said.

She didn't know she was lying when she said it.

* * *

It's totally worth the lie though. When the teacher introduces her to the rest of the class he doesn't say anything about her epilepsy and everyone just smiles and waves. There are no whispers, no funny looks, no sympathy.

It feels *amazing*. Amy misses most of the lesson because she is so busy soaking it up.

The *normalness* of it all is what she's dreamed of ever since she started school. To be like everyone else. Not different or unusual, but just the *same* as them.

But by break time Amy is starting to feel nervous. What if no one likes her? Maybe even if she's totally normal she still won't make any friends? Maybe it wasn't the epilepsy that put her old classmates off all this time … What if it was *her*? What if she had epilepsy *and* she was boring?

The bell rings and the children swarm outside, but Amy lingers at her desk, a sick feeling settling in her stomach.

'Hi Amy,' says a voice behind her. Amy looks round. The girl is tiny, like a pixie, with fair hair, wide brown eyes and a faint accent that tickles Amy's ear. 'I'm Yva. Mr Karlson said I should show you round.'

'Oh, OK. Thank you,' Amy says, trying not to act weird and put her off.

'Come on, then. I'll show you where the loos are. I always need to know where the loo is, don't you?'

Amy nods and follows Yva out of the classroom.

'Where have you moved from?' Yva asks.

'Coventry. My dad got a new job so we had to move.'

'My parents moved here from Poland when I was little, but I've lived here nearly all my life. It's pretty nice round here.'

Yva points out the toilets, the head teacher's office and the dining hall before taking Amy outside into the playground. Lots of children from their class are playing football, some are huddled in small groups talking, while a few others are practising dance moves in the far corner of the playground.

Soon Amy's eyes are drawn to two girls sitting on a bench.

'That's Kara and Tashini,' Yva says. 'That's their bench.'

Amy nods. Every school has its popular children. Amy just wants to be normal. Normal people talk though – they have conversations – and she's hardly said a word to Yva so far!

'Do you like watching that TV show, Pop Explosion?' Amy blurts out, desperate for something to say.

Yva nods, her cheeks pink from the cold. 'My mum lets me watch it sometimes. I like reading best though.'

'Really?'

'Yes, I could read all day, couldn't you?'

'Maybe,' Amy says. 'If the book was really good!'

'I'll lend you some of mine. I've got loads. I save up and spend all my birthday and pocket money on books. You can come round one day and have a look if you want?'

Amy beams. This is what it must be like when you're normal. A new friend and an invitation all in one morning! She'd never been invited to someone's house before. She was left off all the birthday invitations. The parents would make worried excuses to her mum: they couldn't take responsibility if something happened, the other children might get upset if she had a seizure, blah blah blah ...

But not any more.

Her brand new, normal life is just beginning and Amy cannot *wait*.

Chapter Two

A couple of weeks later, Amy and Yva are sprawled on Yva's bedroom floor watching funny videos and laughing, when the doorbell rings.

'Is that your dad already?' Yva asks.

Amy looks at the time and nods. 'Yeah, I think so.'

Yva sighs. 'I wish you could stay forever!'

'Me too!' Amy says and she means it.

She loves Yva's house. It's small and noisy, and crammed full of people all talking at once in a mix of Polish and English. This is her third visit now, and each time she feels like she's been pulled into another far cosier world that smells of nutmeg and fresh washing.

Amy gets up slowly and finds her shoes. Yva's little sister, Greta, bursts in and jumps on Amy.

'Your mum's here, Amy!' she shouts.

'All right, Greta. We heard the bell; you don't need to shout,' says Yva.

Greta pulls a face at her sister and runs off.

My mum? thinks Amy. *Why is my mum picking me up?* Amy jams her shoes on, grabs her bag and rushes down the stairs before her mum can ruin everything.

' ... lovely to meet you, too. Thanks so much for having her.' Amy's mum is chatting to Yva's mum at the door.

'Hi Mum!' Amy shouts, jumping the last three steps, desperate to interrupt before her mum can say anything about her epilepsy. Yva still doesn't know about it and neither does Yva's mum. The note her mum had asked her to give to Ms Kowalska is sitting scrunched up at the bottom of her bag.

'Hello, Amy love. Have you had a nice time?'

'Yes, it's been great,' Amy says, grabbing her mum's arm. 'Thanks for having me, Ms Kowalska! Bye, Yva! See you tomorrow!'

She waves at her friend on the stairs while practically shoving her mum down the path.

'Amy!' her mum complains. 'What is wrong with you?'

'Nothing!' Amy says quickly. 'I'm just hungry. What's for dinner?'

'Oh, your father wanted to do one of his "special" meals so he asked me to collect you.'

Amy grins at her mum. 'Do you think we'll be able to eat it this time?'

'That depends on whether he's learned the difference between tomato puree and chilli puree, I suppose.' Mum rolls her eyes at Amy but she smiles too. They both know it's a good sign that Dad's making dinner. After he lost his job he stopped cooking or doing anything at all really. This new job is a fresh start and so far it's working out for everyone.

Once they're inside the car and driving away, Amy relaxes.

'You should invite Yva round to our house one day,' her mum says. 'I'd like to get to know your new friend a bit more.'

'Yeah, I will,' Amy says and it's true. She will. She just needs to find the right time to explain to Yva about her epilepsy. There's no way her mum won't mention it, so Amy really needs to tell Yva first. She wants to wait a tiny bit longer though, just to be *totally* sure that Yva is truly her friend, whatever happens.

'Why not invite her round next week?' says Mum.

'Maybe. It's just easier to go to Yva's because she lives so close to school,' Amy says, trying to buy more time.

'I suppose so. It must be nice not to do the school run every day.'

'I said I can walk to school, Mum; you don't have to drive me!'

'Hmm,' Mum says, frowning. 'Maybe in a year or two, when you're at secondary school.'

Amy sighs quietly. The epilepsy may be well controlled now, but Mum's worrying about it definitely isn't. If only there was a medicine to take for that.

***

The next afternoon, Mr Karlson explains to them about a project they're going to be doing for the rest of term.

'It's going to be great fun,' he promises. 'As you know, we've been studying some famous characters throughout history up to the present day to see what things we can find out about *them*. Now we're going to focus on each of *you*! Everyone will need to write a short piece filled with lots of interesting facts about themselves. They can be funny or sensible; it's up to you. You could even write a poem or a song if you want, but you will have to read it out in front of everyone at the end-of-term assembly. So make sure you don't write anything too embarrassing!'

A couple of the children start sniggering, but Mr Karlson holds his hands up for quiet.

'I haven't finished yet! As part of this topic there's going to be a group Art competition and the best three groups in our class will have their work displayed in the school foyer where everyone can see it.'

An 'ooh' of excitement ripples around the classroom.

'I hope we're in the same group!' Yva whispers to Amy.

'Me too!' Amy replies.

Mr Karlson pulls names out of a jar until everyone is sorted into a group except Amy.

'Amy! I'm so sorry,' Mr Karlson says when he spies her still sitting at her desk. 'I planned all this before you arrived and I forgot to add your name in.'

'We'll have Amy in our group, Mr Karlson.'

Amy looks up from her desk in shock. It was popular Kara, the girl from the bench. Kara had said her name! Kara had chosen her!

Amy's so flustered she bumps her desk as she gets up and her pencil case falls to the floor. She doesn't even care, though.

'Excellent. Thank you, Kara,' says Mr Karlson.

With all the teams complete, Mr Karlson sends them off to separate tables and brings each group some pictures of different art styles.

'I'm going to give you a bit of time in your groups today to make plans. Remember, this piece of art is all about you, your families and your lives. I want you to think hard about who you are and come up with something brilliant and original. You'll have plenty of time in Art class over the next three weeks to get it done. All right?'

Amy sits quietly at her table, still in shock at being chosen by the coolest girl in class. As well as Kara and Tashini there's a floppy-haired boy called Max in their group who's the only one actually studying the pictures.

'Right, whatever we do it *has* to be *amazing*, right?' Kara says. 'I might go to art college when I'm older so it would look really good if we won.'

'What art do you do?' Max asks her.

Kara sniffs. 'I haven't decided yet. Big stuff. Cool stuff. Like that mural in the town. Hey, we should do one of those!'

'A mural?' Tashini asks. 'Are you sure? That's going to need loads of work.'

'It's a good idea actually,' Max says. 'It would definitely make an impact.'

'I know! I'm a genius!'

'How about we make it more of a collage?' Max suggests, poking his glasses back up his nose. 'That will be more fun than just painting and stuff.'

Kara nods slowly.

'Maybe we could add in family photos and things?' Amy says.

'Yes! That's it, Amy! I knew I was right to choose you,' Kara says, and Amy can't help basking in her approval like a cat rolling in the sunshine.

Kara is so excited by the idea that she calls Mr Karlson over and asks if they can have extra time to work on it.

'You can spend morning break times in the Art room if you need to. But remember, you'll have your written work to do as well.'

'It's fine, Mr Karlson, we really want to win!' Kara says.

'Well, I'm glad to see you're all so excited,' he says, before moving onto the next group.

'Our team is going to make the best art piece the school has ever seen, right?' Kara says.

They all nod, and Amy can feel a nice warm glow of belonging in her belly. It sort of makes up for the fact that she's going to be missing *all* her break times for a while.

Chapter Three

After school, Amy asks her mum for family photos to use in the collage. They have to go up to the loft and find all the albums they didn't unpack when they moved house.

When Dad comes home he discovers them both in the living room, covered in dust and cobwebs, and giggling at a picture of him as a child wearing shorts and sticking his finger up his nose.

'Well, you're not putting that one on your collage!' Dad insists, hiding it behind his back.

'That's all right,' Amy says. 'I can use this one instead!' She shows her dad a picture of him as a baby with chocolate all around his mouth and he chases her around the house for five minutes until she's laughing too much to run any more.

They eat beans on toast on the sofa for supper and keep looking at the albums. Amy loves the ones of her parents when they were young, especially their wedding pictures, but she hides behind a cushion when they get to her baby albums.

'You were so perfect!' Mum says, her voice all gushy. 'I remember looking at you in the hospital and being amazed at how completely perfect you were.'

Although she wasn't *really* perfect, was she? Amy thinks about how she'd started having seizures when she was a toddler and her mum had to give up work so she could stay home and look after her.

Her parents flip quickly through the photos where she has injuries from falling during a seizure, and those where she's wearing a helmet to protect her head, and all the times when she was staying in hospital for tests or treatment.

'You could take in some of these, if you want?' her mum suggests.

'No way!' Amy snaps. 'I told you: I don't want everyone to know I have epilepsy. I'm not going to stick a horrible photo of me looking like that up in the hall, am I?'

'All right, love, it's up to you,' her mum says, closing the album.

'You shouldn't be ashamed of who you are, though, love,' her dad says, frowning.

'I'm not ashamed!' Amy insists, her eyes prickling slightly at the edges. Why can't he understand how much she just wants to be normal for once?

'Of course she's not ashamed,' her mum says. '*You* should be, though, Jack! What on earth were you wearing here?'

Amy's mum points out a picture of Dad looking ridiculous in nineties fashion, and soon the tension is gone. For the rest of the night, they eat ice cream and bicker happily over the best photos to take in to school.

* * *

The next day Yva and Amy are eating their packed lunches together when Tashini and Kara come over to *their* table.

Amy nearly chokes on her juice but manages to swallow it before she can cough all over Kara and Tashini, and ruin her life forever.

'Hey, Amy,' Kara says. 'I asked Mr Karlson if we could make a start on our project. Do you want to come with us?'

'Oh! OK, yes. I can come,' Amy says, stumbling over her words as she packs up her lunch.

'Have fun, Amy!' Yva says.

Amy nods. 'I'll see you later in class?'

'Of course.'

Amy follows Tashini and Kara across the dining hall, trying to look calm and act like she hangs out with the cool kids every day.

Then she trips on a table leg and nearly falls over.

Her cheeks flame.

'Careful Amy!' Kara says, grabbing her elbow to steady her.

'Sorry, thanks,' she stammers.

'Don't worry about it,' Tashini says with a careless wave of her hand. 'This hall is way too crowded. My sister says there's a huge cafeteria at the secondary school with a salad bar and everything.'

'Cool,' Amy says. 'I love salad.'

Kara smiles. 'You're so sweet, Amy.'

But the way she says it almost makes it sound like the opposite.

Max is waiting for them in the classroom with a box full of photos. Kara and Tashini rummage through them giggling and Amy can see Max's ears turning redder and redder.

'Max, you are so funny!' Tashini says. 'Look at you.'

She holds up a photo of Max dressed as a pirate with two missing front teeth and a wonky fringe.

'Yeah, yeah ... Where are your pictures, then?' Max demands, and Tashini and Kara lay their photos on the table.

Hard as he tries though, he can't find a single embarrassing one. All the photos are full of smiling, happy, fashionably-dressed people.

'These are so boring!' he tells them.

'I'm not letting everyone at school laugh at me!' Kara says.

'But this project is supposed to be about who we are!' Max exclaims.

'Yeah, and everyone knows we're perfect, Max!'

Max sighs and looks at Amy. 'What about you?'

Amy hands over her own pictures and he flicks through them, grinning. 'These are great! I love the ones of your grandparents and you when you were little.'

'Thanks, I don't really remember them much so it's nice to have pictures.'

Kara gives them a half-hearted glance and then sniffs.

'What else are we going to use for this collage then, apart from photos?' she demands.

'We should decide on the background first before we worry about the collage,' Max says.

Kara flicks him an annoyed look.

'What about trees?' Amy suggests. 'You know, like family trees?'

'*Boring*!' Kara says. 'Come on, Amy! It needs to be original! Everyone is going to be doing family trees, aren't they?'

'Are they? Sorry,' Amy mutters.

'Well, what do you suggest, then?' Max asks Kara.

'I can't do everything, can I? I'm more about the big picture.'

They sit in silence for a few minutes and Amy's eyes wander all over the Art room. There are wet paintings on some of the tables, resting on old newspaper. She picks at some with her finger.

'Hey, what about newspaper?' Amy says. 'We could print off some headlines that tie in with when we were born and stuff like that?'

'Yeah, we could even make up our own newspapers with our pictures included like they're news stories or something?' Max suggests.

Tashini taps her lip for a minute. 'A black and white background would be cool, especially if we did a bright graffiti-type border, maybe?'

'My brother does graffiti at college! I could ask him for some tips.' Max says.

'Now that's more like it!' Kara says, with a beaming smile. 'I knew we could do it if we put our minds to it! This is going to be amazing!'

Max rolls his eyes and Amy has to cover her smile with her hand.

Chapter Four

'I'm going to take you to school today,' her dad says over breakfast the next day.

'I can walk to school, you don't have to drive me,' Amy says, munching her third piece of toast.

'Ah, but what if I want to spend time with my lovely and talented daughter before she grows up and leaves me?' he asks.

'All right then, if you like,' Amy says, giggling at his silliness. *Dad's so much happier since he got this new job,* Amy thinks. *Last year he barely spoke at all, let alone made jokes.*

'How very gracious of you!' Dad says, putting his cereal bowl in the sink.

'Hey, maybe you could be my permanent chauffeur when I'm rich and famous?' Amy suggests.

'And maybe you could get in the car before we're permanently late!'

They laugh and joke all the way to school, but when they're parked up outside, Dad asks her to wait a minute.

'Look, I know moving away and starting a new school must have been difficult for you but I just wanted to say I'm really proud of how well you've coped.'

'Dad, it's fine … ' Amy begins, but he holds his hand up to stop her.

'I know you haven't had it easy with your epilepsy, but you never stop being brave and it makes me so happy to see you getting involved and making friends, despite everything.' He pulls her in for a hug and kisses the top of her head.

'I love you, Amykins; don't forget it,' he says, as she gets out of the car.

'Love you too, Dad,' she says, wishing she was really the daughter he thought she was.

* * *

Amy and Yva are so busy catching up in the playground, they have to run to avoid being late. Everyone is gathered around Kara's desk.

'So, we're all going to have pizza at *Giuseppe's*,' she says. 'And then my mum's rented out a *whole* screen at the cinema and I get to turn on the projector for the film and everything.'

Yva makes a puzzled face at Amy, but she doesn't know what's going on either, so she just shrugs.

'It's going to be the *best* birthday party ever,' Kara promises. 'Mum says I can invite ten friends,' she adds, and you can almost feel the thrill of anticipation in the room.

'I've already got my invitation,' Tashini says, which means there's only nine spaces left now.

'I'm still making my mind up about the rest,' Kara says, gazing coolly around the room at all the desperate faces. 'But I'll let you know.'

She slides into her chair as Mr Karlson comes in and bellows at them all to sit down and be quiet.

It takes a while before the whispers finally stop. Amy knows everyone's still thinking about the party, instead of the sums written on the board, because that's exactly what *she's* doing.

Imagine if the first birthday party she ever went to was Kara's? A pizza and cinema party with a girl who was super popular and cool?

Amy desperately wants to be part of something special and fun instead of forever standing on the sidelines, but what are the chances she'll be one of the chosen few? Kara said they were friends now, but she's still just the new girl, isn't she?

Amy sighs and starts working out the answers to the sums.

Yva nudges her and passes a piece of paper across the desk.

> We can go to the cinema in the holidays!
> xxx

Amy reads it on her lap.

She smiles at Yva and nods. *It would probably be more fun going with Yva anyway,* Amy thinks. She doesn't have to try to be a certain way all the time with Yva. Yva likes her just as she is. Maybe she even likes her enough that Amy could tell her the truth?

Amy gnaws at her lower lip and decides to wait just a little bit longer to be extra sure.

Chapter Five

Two days later, Amy finds a sparkly envelope sitting on her desk. She looks over at Yva who smiles. The smile doesn't quite reach her eyes, but Amy is too excited to notice. When she rips the envelope open she finds a printed card with her name on, inviting her to Kara's birthday party.

Amy squeals, runs over to Kara and hugs her.

'Calm down, Amy; it's just a party!' Kara says with a small frown.

Amy coughs and tries to control her excitement. 'Yeah, course. It's just nice because I'm new here and everything.'

'Well, Suri and Jack are busy that day so there are a couple of extra places and you're part of my art team now, so why not?'

'You could ask Yva too if there's another spare place? She's really nice.'

Kara makes a face. 'It's my party, Amy. I decide who's coming!'

'Right, of course,' Amy wants to sink into the ground. Why had she said that? What a fool! 'Sorry. And thank you, I'm really looking forward to it.'

'Yeah, me too! See you later for Art, all right?'

Amy nods and hurries back to her desk before Kara changes her mind altogether.

* * *

Amy can't get any work done all morning because she's too busy thinking about the party. She's actually really and truly going! Her heart skips a little with every beat and she has to concentrate hard to stop herself from smiling *all* the time.

She's been right to hide her epilepsy from everyone. She has friends now, Art projects, party invitations and everything she dreamed about all those long afternoons lying on the sofa after a seizure.

At break time, her group gathers in the Art room to start their project. It's mainly Max and Amy who do all the work, pasting old newspapers on to the huge white card on the walls. Kara and Tashini are too busy discussing what they're going to wear to the party.

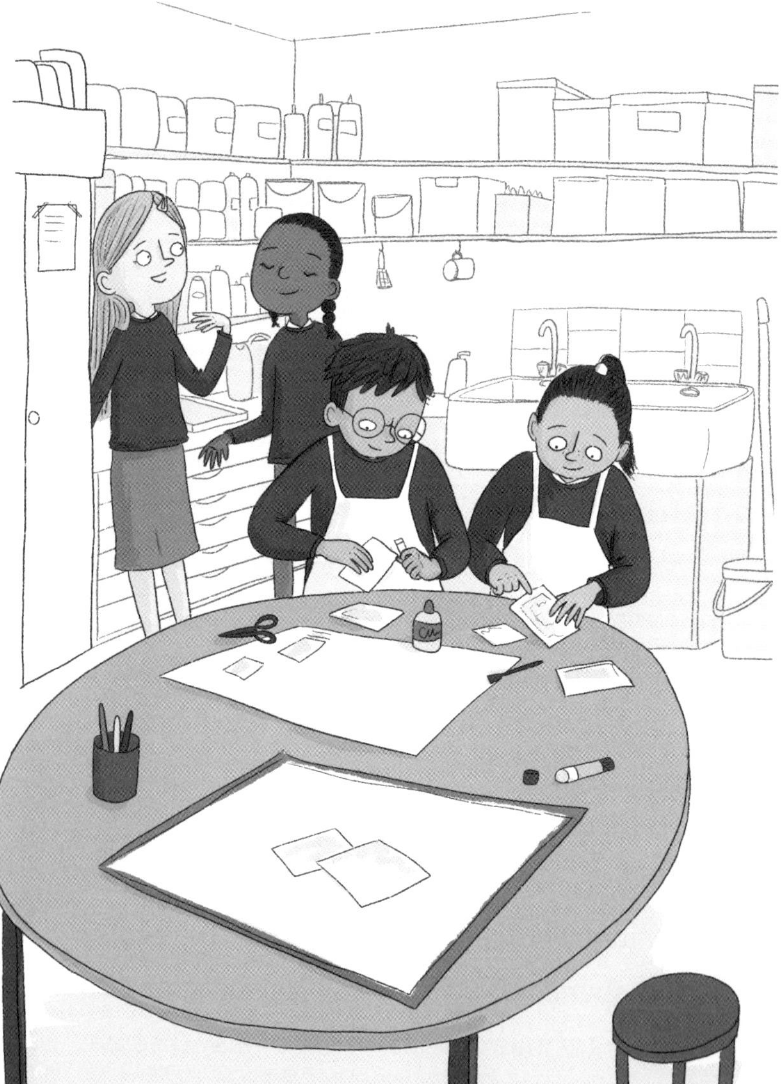

It would be annoying if Amy wasn't enjoying herself so much. Max is really fun and their project is definitely starting to take shape. Maybe they'll even win. Her parents would be so proud to see her work in the school foyer!

She finds Yva sitting at their table eating lunch and sinks down into the chair next to her, feeling tired but happy.

'Hi, sorry I didn't see you at break. Kara wanted us to work on our project again.'

'It's fine,' Yva says, peeling her tangerine. 'You must be excited about the party?'

'I am! I can't believe she invited me.'

'Why not? You're friends now, aren't you?'

'Yeah, but I haven't been here very long.' Amy bites into her tuna roll. 'I wish you were coming too,' she says.

'I wouldn't want to go,' Yva says.

'What? Why not? Everyone wants to go.'

Yva shrugs her shoulders. 'I don't really like those girls; they're not very nice.'

Amy swallows her mouthful and looks at Yva.

'But they're the most popular girls in school!'

'So? I don't really care about being popular. Do you?'

'Yes, a bit. I mean, I've never really been popular before so it's exciting.'

'OK. Just be careful,' says Yva.

'Careful?'

'When they like you it's fine but when they stop … '

'Why would they stop liking me?' Amy demands.

'I don't know. They probably won't.'

'Then why say it?'

Yva shakes her head. 'Just forget I said anything.'

But Amy can't. Yva's words have poked at the very thing she's most afraid of and now she's furious. 'Maybe you're just jealous?'

'I'm not jealous, Amy, I just don't want you to get hurt. You're my best friend.'

'Yeah, well, maybe I've found some new friends!' Amy grabs her lunch and marches away.

She doesn't look back. The sight of Yva sitting there all alone might make her cry.

Chapter Six

'Who's Kara?' Amy's mum says when she tells her about the party on the way home.

'She's in my project group in Art. She's really cool.'

'Well, it sounds like a very fancy party.'

'I know. I can't wait!'

'Is Yva going?'

'No. She wasn't invited.'

'Oh, that's a shame.'

'Yeah.' Amy doesn't want to think about Yva. Not now. 'Only ten people are going to the party though, Mum. I can't believe Kara picked me when I'm new and everything.'

Even better than feeling normal is feeling chosen, Amy decides. It makes her feel warm deep inside.

Amy's mum nods. 'I'll need to have a word with Kara's mum just in case. Is there a phone number on the invitation?'

'Mum! I don't want everyone knowing. I told you.'

'Amy, don't be silly! I have to tell her if she's going to be responsible for you all day!'

'Why are you ruining everything?' Amy shouts. 'I get my first invitation to a party – the coolest party ever – and you want to ruin it for me!'

'How am I ruining it?'

'Because all you can think about is my epilepsy! Can't you ever just forget about it – even for a minute – and let me enjoy something?'

Amy's mum bites her lip and glares at the road ahead.

Amy stares out of the window wondering how she's managed to fall out with two of her favourite people over a birthday party in just one day.

Chapter Seven

When the big day finally comes, Amy is determined to enjoy every minute. She is *not* going to think about how much she misses Yva.

Kara is my friend now, thinks Amy. Amy has spent lots of time with her this week, and she even sat on the bench in the playground with her and Tashini one lunchtime. Yva is probably just jealous that they like her more.

'Amy!' Her mum calls up the stairs. 'Are you ready?'

'Coming!' Amy shouts back, grabbing her jacket and shoes and running down to meet her.

'You look nice,' Mum says.

'Thanks.' Amy has spent some of her birthday money on a smart top. Buying new clothes for a party is all part of her dream.

'Have you got the card and present?' asks Mum.

'Yep, in my bag.'

'Let's go then.'

Amy follows her mum out to the car. She can tell her mum's trying to be extra nice, but she still feels a bit betrayed.

Her mum had phoned Kara's mum yesterday and had a 'little chat' with her.

Amy had sobbed when she found out, but her mum promised everything was fine.

'Kara's mum understood that you're a bit embarrassed and don't like to talk about your epilepsy,' she'd told Amy last night. 'She promised not to say a word to anyone.'

Amy wanted to believe her mum, but a little part of her was scared they'd all be furious at her when she arrived, and she'd have to go home again.

But Kara is smiling and waving when she walks up to the restaurant and Amy almost melts with relief. It's all fine! Kara doesn't know!

'I hope you have a nice time, love,' Amy's mum says.

'Thank you!' Amy says, reaching in for a hug.

Her mum looks surprised but gives her a big squeeze and a relieved smile.

'Come on, Amy!' Tashini calls. Amy waves her mum goodbye and rushes inside after her friends, ready for the fun to begin.

* * *

Amy is amazed how noisy parties are! Their table is a whirlwind of chaos as everyone eats and talks and laughs and shouts and jumps up to chase each other around the table every now and then.

58

It's all a bit overwhelming for Amy, who doesn't really know everyone and is used to a bit more calm and quiet. Luckily, she's sitting next to Max who tells her funny stories about his pet dog, Mr Paws, but it's quite hard to hear him over the racket. Kara's mum is keeping an eye on them all from a nearby table, but she looks exhausted already. At least they'd have to be quiet in the cinema, Amy thought.

Except they aren't. Kara's mum has rented out the whole screen so there are no other people in there with them, and twenty minutes after they've sat down nearly everyone is running around the cinema instead of watching the film.

Kara doesn't seem to care, even though she'd made a huge fuss about pressing the button on the projector and went on and on about how this was her favourite film ever. Amy sits with Max and Kara's mum and tries to enjoy herself, but it's hard.

Amy can't help feeling disappointed. *This was going to be the best day of my life,* she thinks.

But it's more fun (and much less noisy) going round to Yva's house and just hanging out.

'What's up?' Max asks her, as she fidgets in her seat.

Amy shrugs. 'This is the first birthday party I've been to. It's just not what I was expecting.'

'I've been to about ten and it's all about the goody-bag. Trust me.'

'Goody-bag?'

'Yeah, we all get a bag of sweets and things to take home at the end. Didn't you know?'

'No!' Amy says, a glimmer of excitement in her voice.

'Yeah. Sometimes there's even a book inside.'

'Cool,' Amy says. If it was a book maybe she could give it to Yva. She could say sorry and ask if they can be friends again.

When the popcorn fight gets completely out of hand, the cinema attendant storms in and makes everyone sit down and watch the film. Maybe because they're all exhausted that's what they do, and Amy can finally relax into her chair.

She's going to make it up with Yva, she decides. She will explain to her about her epilepsy and why she'd been so excited about a silly party. Yva will understand. She is one of the kindest people Amy knows.

Amy tries to concentrate on the film but her eyes are sore and there's a pain in her head.

She needs to go outside.

Now.

She gets up and moves into the aisle. Her legs feel wobbly and everything looks really hazy.

'Amy? Amy!'

But Amy can't hear them when they call her name. She can't hear anything.

Chapter Eight

'You have to go in, love,' Mum says after they've been sitting in the car outside school for ten minutes.

'It's going to be awful,' Amy mutters.

'The other kids might gossip for a few days, but they were probably just a bit scared when they saw your seizure. Everyone will forget about it soon enough. It's best that it's out in the open now, Amy, you know that.'

It's definitely out in the open. Having a seizure in front of half her class in the middle of a cinema has made sure of that.

She doesn't really remember any of it, of course. She never does. Mum had to explain it to her hours later when she was lying on the sofa recovering. Every seizure is like a tiny electric shock in her brain. It makes her muscles jerk and shudder really hard, and afterwards her whole body aches and her head pounds and pounds like a drum.

But she usually felt better after a long sleep and a day on the sofa wrapped in a duvet, watching her favourite shows on television.

Not this time, though. Amy had spent the whole of Sunday worrying because she knew she had to go into school on Monday, and everyone would know the truth about her.

Sitting in the car now, Amy just wishes and wishes that she'd told Yva the truth ages ago, right at the beginning. Now Yva will find out from gossip and know that Amy had kept it a secret from her.

She's messed up her one chance to have a real friend and she really misses Yva and her cosy house. She even misses Greta's over-enthusiastic shouting.

'Amy?' Her mum prompts her again.

'All right! I'm going.' Amy slams her way out of the car and stalks into school. She can feel eyes on her already.

No doubt Kara hadn't wasted any time spreading the gossip all around the school. Amy bites her lip, keeps her head down and walks as fast as possible to her classroom.

'Good morning Amy!' Mr Karlson says.

'Morning, sir,' Amy whispers, sitting down quickly.

The classroom starts to fill up. Amy can hear the children's excited whispering when they see her but she keeps her eyes firmly fixed on her desk.

'Hello, Amy,' Yva says, sitting down next to her.

'Hi, Yva!' Amy wants to talk to her, to apologize and explain, but Yva takes a book out of her bag and starts reading.

She doesn't want to talk to Amy, why should she? Yva is just being polite as always.

Mr Karlson calls for quiet to take the register and Amy ignores the whispering when he calls her name. *This is what it's going to be like from now on,* Amy thinks. *I'll just have to get used to it.*

* * *

It's a long morning of side looks and more whispers. When the bell finally rings, Amy nips to the bathroom to avoid everyone and then hurries to the Art room to carry on with the project.

Adding to the collage will help distract her, and hopefully Max won't mind her being there. He doesn't have to talk to her if he doesn't want to.

But Max isn't in the Art room when she gets there. Kara and Tashini are.

'Where's Max?' Amy asks.

'He's sick. He's going to be off all week,' Kara says.

'Oh.' Amy goes to get art supplies from the cupboard but Kara gets in her way.

'Listen, Amy, don't you think you should keep away from the project now?' she says.

'What? Why?'

'Isn't it obvious?'

Amy swallows, hard. 'Look, I'm sorry about what happened at your party Kara, but ... '

'It's not about the party.'

'Really?'

'No. It's not your fault if you have seizures, is it? But what if you had another one?' Kara asks. 'The collage's nearly finished and it looks amazing. What if you fell and spilled paint on it or messed it up somehow?'

Amy can feel her face getting hot. 'But my medication works. I only had a seizure because I didn't get much sleep the night before and forgot to take my medicine!'

'But you can't *know* for sure that you won't have another one, can you?' Tashini asks.

'Maybe not a hundred per cent,' Amy admits.

'So why risk it? Do you really want to ruin it for the rest of us after all the work we've done? We might even win, but not if you mess it up!'

Disappointment blooms inside Amy's heart. She doesn't want to stop working on the project; it's become her favourite part of school. But what if Kara is right?

'There's not much left to do now so just let us finish it off, all right?' Tashini says.

Amy nods because she can't speak past the lump in her throat.

'Great,' Kara says. 'And now you can enjoy your break times so that's good, isn't it?'

Amy nods again and slips out of the classroom quickly.

What good is break time when she doesn't have anyone to spend it with?

Chapter Nine

'Amy! Wait behind after class please,' Mr Karlson says just as the bell goes and the other children rush for the door.

Amy sighs, packs up her bag slowly and heads for his desk. It was probably more bad news.

'So, Amy, how are you doing? Are you feeling better after your seizure?'

'Yes, sir.'

'Good,' he says, smiling at her. 'I noticed you haven't been working on your collage the last couple of days?'

'Kara … I mean, *we*, decided it was best if I let the others finish it off,' she tells him, trying to pretend she's fine about it even though it still hurts.

Mr Karlson nods. 'I see. But if you're not working on your Art project you should have plenty of time to complete your personal writing and … ' he opens the workbook on his desk and waves a hand over her messy, crossed-out scrawl. 'This really isn't good enough.'

Amy bites her lip.

'The assembly is on Friday, Amy.'

'I'm sorry, sir, I just … ' she trails off.

'Well, you're not the only one struggling. I want you to go to the library tomorrow at break and work with another student, all right?'

'Yes, sir.'

'I think you are capable of writing something much better than this Amy. I want to be proud of you and I'm sure your parents do too, so please make an effort.'

'I'll try,' she says with a long sigh.

Mr Karlson smiles. 'Thank you, you can go home now.'

Amy nods and walks slowly towards the door, her shoulders hunched low as if she is carrying a bucketful of bricks instead of a school bag.

* * *

At break the next day Amy is sitting in the library with her workbook open when Yva walks in.

'Did Mr Karlson tell you to come here?'

Amy nods.

Yva sits down next to her and grabs her workbook from her bag.

'I'm glad I'm working with you,' Amy says.

Yva gives her a tiny smile. 'So, what are you struggling with?'

Amy sighs. 'Everything. I hate writing about myself.'

'It's really hard, isn't it? I much prefer writing stories about other people.'

'Yeah. I'm so boring there's nothing much to say.'

'Let me read what you've written,' says Yva.

'And I'll read yours?'

'OK.'

They pick up each other's books.

'Oh, Amy,' Yva says with a tiny waver in her voice.

'What?'

'You wrote: *I am Yva's friend, Yva is my best friend, I love going to Yva's house* – and then you crossed them all out!'

Amy bites her thumbnail. She'd forgotten about crossing them out.

Yva reaches across and points at the last line of her own writing: *Amy is my best friend, I like her very much* – and there is no crossing out.

'But ... ' Amy stares at Yva. 'You haven't spoken to me for ages!'

Yva shrugs. 'I thought *you* didn't want to speak to me.'

'So ... are we still friends?' Amy asks.

'Do you want us to be?'

'Yes! Yes, more than anything. I'm so sorry I was horrible to you; I know you weren't jealous really. I was just scared that you were right about Kara and the others.'

'Why were you so scared?'

Amy sighs. 'Because at my last school I didn't have any friends. I had seizures at school almost every week and everyone was a bit scared of them, so they didn't want to hang out with me.'

'Is that why you didn't tell me about your epilepsy?'

Amy nods. 'I wanted to! Lots of times, but I was afraid you wouldn't like me any more.'

'You silly thing!' Yva says. 'Friends like each other, whatever. That's why they're friends!'

Amy shakes her head. 'Not always. I thought Kara was my friend but now she doesn't even want me to work on our Art project any more.'

'What? That's not fair.'

Amy shrugs. 'It doesn't matter. Maybe she's right. If I had another seizure I could spoil the collage.'

'That's rubbish. Anyone could fall over and spill paint on it!'

'I suppose so,' Amy says. 'Anyway, you were right about her, I guess. I should have listened to you.'

'Maybe there are some things you have to learn the hard way,' Yva says.

'Or I could just listen to you from now on!'

'Well, I am very wise,' Yva says, and Amy can't help laughing. With Ms Chowdary glaring at them, they decide it might be wise to leave the library before they get into trouble.

It's only later, on the way home, that Amy wonders if Mr Karlson had read her crossings out too and sent Yva to the library deliberately. She thinks maybe he had, and that he might well be her favourite teacher ever.

Chapter Ten

Everything is better now that Yva and Amy are friends again – proper friends this time, with no more secrets.

She misses working on her Art project, and everyone else in her class is still mostly avoiding her, but she's got a friend coming over to do homework for the first time ever, so that's something. Her mum is so pleased she even manages not to be *too* embarrassing when she greets Yva.

Upstairs in Amy's bedroom they get out their workbooks.

'This is so hard!' Amy complains. 'What am I supposed to write?'

'Well, you missed out something important.'

'What?'

'Your epilepsy, of course!'

Amy sighs. 'I don't want to talk about that.'

'Why?'

'Because once people know that I have epilepsy that's all they can see. I stop being Amy who likes Art and Music and become Amy the Epileptic Girl.'

Yva nods. 'That must be really hard.'

'It is.'

'But maybe if you spoke about it more and people understood it better, then it would stop being such a big thing?'

Amy huffs. It's easy for Yva to say that, isn't it?

'Well, you've left out one of the most important things about you!'

'What?'

'That you're from Poland!'

'No one wants to know about that,' Yva says.

'That's not true. I'd love to know more about it.'

'Yeah, well, you're the only one!'

'Do you go there for holidays?'

'Yeah, my uncle and aunts live there and we go back for Christmas sometimes. They usually have lots more snow than us and we have a great big feast on Christmas Eve with all the family.'

'That sounds lovely,' says Amy, who's used to having small, quiet Christmases.

They get so caught up in talking about Poland and Christmas and planning the perfect feast that they forget to do any work. When Yva's mum arrives they have to quickly promise to meet up at break time tomorrow and definitely, absolutely get their writing done.

Chapter Eleven

'Amy!'

Amy turns around and smiles when she sees Max walk into class. He's been off for ages and she's missed seeing him.

'Hi Max, are you feeling better?'

'Yeah, it was just my asthma playing up,' he says. 'What's happening with the collage? It has to be handed in tomorrow.'

'I haven't been working on it. Kara and Tashini said they were going to finish it off.'

'But they haven't done anything,' Max says. 'I just went to check.'

'What? That doesn't make any sense.'

'Oi, Kara!' Max shouts across the classroom. 'Why haven't you finished off the collage?'

Kara frowns and flicks her hair back. 'Me and Tashini were too busy so we had to leave it.'

'But I could have finished it off!' Amy says. 'Why didn't you just tell me?'

'It's just a silly collage. Who cares?'

'I thought you were desperate to win?' Max says. 'Because you were going to art college or something?'

'Yeah, well, I changed my mind. Me and Tashini are going to be in a girl band instead, so we don't have time for art and stuff.'

'Well thanks for dropping us in it, Kara,' Max snaps.

'I'm sorry, Max. It's my fault,' Amy says, close to tears.

'No, it's not. Those two just like causing trouble.'

'I shouldn't have listened to them.'

'We can still finish it, Amy, if we go at break and lunchtime today,' Max says.

'I can't! I'm supposed to be writing my personal story with Yva at break. It's still not finished.'

* * *

'You should go with Max,' Yva says.

'But I'll get into trouble if my writing isn't finished!'

'I've got an idea about that.'

'Really?'

'Yes, I'll sort everything out at break and we can practise tonight at my house!'

'Practise?'

Yva smiles. 'Don't worry, it will be fun! Probably.'

Chapter Twelve

At the end-of-term assembly, Amy can see her parents in the audience, sitting next to Yva's mum and her babcia. There's a fluttering of nerves in Amy's tummy but she can see Yva smiling at her from the other side of the stage, and that helps.

Eventually it's Yva's turn to go on stage and she walks out and stands in the middle. But instead of reading her speech out like everyone else, Amy starts talking from the edge of the stage.

'This is my friend Yva. She likes cats, soup and reading. She is kind and funny, and makes me laugh.'

Yva takes over as Amy walks on to the stage to stand beside her, just as they had practised.

'This is my friend Amy. She likes Art, Music and grizzly bears. She is brave, generous and fun.'

The two girls smile at each other.

'She is my friend,' they say at the same time.

Next Amy tells everyone that Yva is from Poland and how she has a babcia instead of a grandma, and celebrates Christmas on the 24th December.

Then Yva explains about Amy's epilepsy. She describes what it's like to have a seizure, explaining that although they look a bit scary, seizures are usually over quickly. Yva then talks about how other people can help if they see a seizure, just by staying with Amy and keeping her safe.

'She is my friend,' they say again when they've finished. 'Because friends are friends whatever.'

There's a burst of applause from the audience and Amy can see her mum is crying and Yva's babcia is cheering in Polish, and she looks over at Yva who can't stop smiling.

When all the children have finished speaking, Mr Karlson walks onto stage.

'Thank you to everyone who came today. As well as working on their very brilliant personal essays, the children have also been involved in group Art projects. Three of the projects have been specially chosen to be displayed in the school foyer, so do please go and have a look before you go home!'

Amy is almost scared to go into the foyer. She and Max had worked so hard trying to finish their collage yesterday, but with a whole week wasted there hadn't really been enough time to do everything.

Eventually Yva has to drag her in there.

'Amy!' Max comes running over, his face so excited Amy knows at once that their project must be there. 'We did it! Look!'

Amy follows him through the crush to the far wall where their collage has been hung up. It looks amazing and Amy's heart does a weird jumpy thing when she sees it.

Soon her family, Yva and her family, and Max's mum come and stand with them and admire the collage they made.

Among the newspaper headlines there are the words *epilepsy* and *asthma* because Max said it had to be honest. The best art always is.

Mr Karlson comes over to congratulate them all and says they did a brilliant job helping people understand more about them. Amy's dad whispers in her ear how proud he is, and for once Amy actually feels proud of herself.

Max points out the label with their names typed on.

'I guess the judges must have felt sorry for you two!' Kara says in a low voice.

'Actually, Kara,' Mr Karlson says, 'The judges were impressed by their imagination and hard work.'

'But Tashini and I worked on it too and our names aren't even on there!'

'Yes, they are,' Amy says, and she taps their names at the bottom.

'Yeah, well, who cares anyway?' Kara flounces off, but Amy is too happy to care.

'You should think about going to art college,' Max says. 'I'm going to.'

'Maybe I will,' Amy says, smiling at him.

'I think I'm going to go travelling when I finish school,' Yva says. 'We could go together?'

'That sounds fun!' Amy says, squeezing Yva's hand.

Somehow, despite all her mistakes, Amy has two friends who like her just as she is, and a future she can be excited about.

Finally, it feels as if Amy's shed the bubble wrap that has surrounded her for so long. Everything around her looks just a little bit brighter now.

95

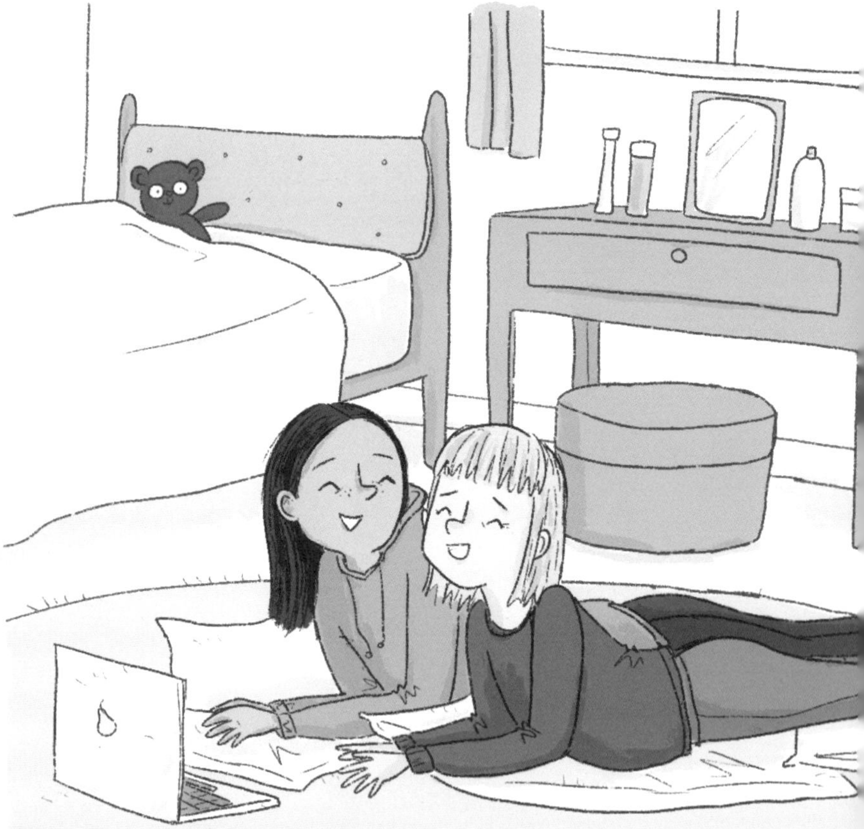